PREPARE
THE WAY

PREPARE THE WAY

CULTIVATING A HEART FOR GOD IN ADVENT

PAMELA C. HAWKINS

UPPER ROOM BOOKS®
NASHVILLE

Cover design: Bruce Gore, Gorestudio.Inc.
Cover photo: Shutterstock
Interior design: Perfect Type, Nashville, Tennessee

LIBRARY OF CONGRESS CATALOGING-IN-PUBLICATION DATA

Names: Hawkins, Pamela C., author.

Title: Prepare the way : cultivating a heart for God in Advent / Pamela C. Hawkins.

Description: Nashville : Upper Room Books, 2016.

Identifiers: LCCN 2016005506| ISBN 9780835815697 (print) | ISBN 9780835815703

(mobi) | ISBN 9780835815710 (epub)

Subjects: LCSH: Advent—Prayers and devotions.

Classification: LCC BV40 .H385 2016 | DDC 242/.332--dc23

LC record available at https://lccn.loc.gov/2016005506

In memory of my beloved RAY
and in deep respect and love
for my sons ERICK and PHILIP
who have all been
tireless companions
on my walk with God

Contents

Introduction

For much of my life, the shape and story of Christmas formed around readings from the four Gospels. And within the boundaries of the Gospel accounts of Jesus' arrival into the world, I pinned my most vivid Christmas imagination against Luke's Gospel. Like in a child's kaleidoscope, each year the colorful fragments from other Gospel readings may have come into view momentarily, but my overall faith perspective of the significance of Jesus' birth came into focus only at the reading of the second chapter of Luke.

Like many others of my generation, the existence and meager celebration of Advent in my church ensured that I did not notice it until I was in my twenties. Readings from the Prophets were uncommon in my church upbringing, and although I now know that some of my favorite Christmas hymn lyrics have a prophetic grounding, I had no idea of this in my early years. In my home church, we seemed to leap in worship from Thanksgiving to Christmas Eve, bypassing the elegant and essential bridge of Advent built on God's prophetic word. But since that time, I have discovered and grown close to the words of Isaiah and other prophets whom God called to speak truth and promise to God's people, even when they blatantly and destructively lived outside of their covenant with God.

So powerful in message and beauty, the words of God's prophets shine through the darkness of the people of their times as well as through our contemporary darkness that descends when we, God's people, continue to stray from covenantal faithfulness to God. To approach Christmas only by way of the Advent Gospel readings will leave us ill-equipped to live in the post-Christmas world that is not all stars and angels, but is, in fact, rife with both destruction and possibility. Humanity cannot take Advent and God's coming among us to heart if we bypass the prophets. God's people struggled mightily with faithfulness and faithlessness. Their struggle and lack of discernment often brought dire and desperate consequences. Yet through the cacophony of pleas, arrogance, and wars, God's prophets spoke to the people of a redemptive future of joy, kindness, and peace—all made possible by God's steadfast love born into the world. When we allow God's prophets to speak a word to us, alongside those of the Gospel writers, we discover an even more stellar and glorious gift in the manger: Because of the darkness, the Light comes to us. Because of sin's death-dealing ways, the life-giving ways of faith in Jesus the Christ can reassure us that "all things are possible" because God is with us.

For me, Advent's message finds its integrity by placing the Prophets next to the Gospels—darkness against light, despair against hope, fear against love. So this book will not neglect the prophets who proclaim humanity's need for salvation and the expanse of God's desire for our redemption through Christ. This little book accords Prophet and Gospel equal honor. I pray you will find that God speaks to you in fresh, meaningful ways as you enter into this study, which is grounded in and born of God's holy word for the Advent season.

How to Use This Book

First and foremost, I designed this book for use as a personal Advent resource. A reader may or may not choose to participate in a small-group study. If you are not in a group, it will be best to begin your reading on the Monday before the first Sunday of Advent and follow each day's reading guide so that you will complete Day Seven of each week on a Sunday in Advent. This will help you prepare for the upcoming weekly worship experience. But do not worry if you must read on a different weekly schedule because you may use the daily readings and reflections in whatever pattern suits your schedule.

Small-Group Participants and Leaders

For persons who wish to use *Prepare the Way* in a small-group format, a Leader's Guide begins on page 95 for use during the weekly group sessions. The leader will determine and communicate the weekly reading schedule to group participants so that all read in the same rhythm. Again, if possible, it will be best if small groups plan to begin reading and meeting for Week One during the week before the first Sunday of Advent.

Sunday School Classes

If members of a class or group wish to follow *Prepare the Way* during Advent, leaders will find that they can easily adapt the sixty-minute small-group study for use in a forty-five to fifty-minute time frame. Members will need a copy of *Prepare the Way* before the first class meeting to read and reflect on the assignment before a class gathers for discussion.

Weekly Material to Be Read and Prepared

Daily material does not require extensive preparation time, varying from ten to fifteen minutes to no more than thirty minutes. Allow approximately one hour for the completion of a whole week's readings and reflections in one sitting.

Each week follows the same pattern and begins with a single word inspired by lectionary readings for the week from the prophet Isaiah and the Gospel reading from Matthew. Based on the week's theme word, each week's daily readings and exercises include the following:

Day One: A reflection on the theme word; an Advent Invocation; and reflection through a sentence completion exercise.

Day Two: A reading of an Advent article followed by reflection questions.

Day Three: An Advent Prayer of Intercession followed by an invitation to remain in intercessory prayer through a bidding prayer exercise.

Day Four: A selection from the prophet Isaiah, followed by a set of reflection questions connecting the reading to the week's theme word.

Day Five: A selection from the Gospel of Matthew, followed by a set of reflection questions connecting the reading to the week's theme word.

Day Six: A guide to the spiritual practice of *lectio divina*, sacred reading, using verses from one of the week's two scripture passages.

Day Seven: A reflection exercise prompting personal responses to questions about how the theme word influences faithful living in the world, closing with an Advent Benediction.

Resources and Materials Needed

Participants need only a copy of *Prepare the Way*, and, if desired, a journal or notebook in which to write prayers and responses. If preferred, participants may make brief notes in their copy of *Prepare the Way*. *Prepare the Way* includes scripture texts. But if readers prefer a translation other than the New Revised Standard Version, they will want to use their own Bible.

Before You Begin

Each time you sit down to begin reading this material, take time to get comfortable and to breathe deeply. The weeks leading up to Christmas are typically overfilled with busyness and holiday commitments that are stacked upon our too-full lives. Remember that simply by committing to this study, reading, and prayer, you have already made room for the coming of Christ, and in doing so, you have begun to cultivate a new and refreshed heart for God. Remember that you are a beloved child of God, and set your expectation that God has a word for you through the readings and prayers of this study. Just as God met me through the writing process of this book, I trust that God waits for you in the reading of it. So breathe, prepare your heart, watch for God's word for you, and begin.

The Way of Peace

Advent Invocation

O Peace,
that long, sacred horizon
where violent dust settles
onto heaven's gentle calm.
You are the prophet's cry
and the angel's midnight song,
a lullaby for the wolf
and promise to the lamb.
Holy Peace,
given, yet still sought,
enfold God's earth this Advent,
warming hearts
until every sharp edge curves,
smoothed and burnished,
toward you.
Amen.

Using a notebook, journal, or space below, complete the following sentences:

- I am most aware of God's peace when

- I am in need of God's peace for

- My life has the most peace when

- During Advent and at Christmas, I am most reminded of God's peace when

DAY TWO

Find a quiet place and time to read the following reflection. To deepen and slow your reading into a more prayerful experience, consider reading aloud.

She slunk toward our porch like a night spy sent to get the lay of the land. Cautious and hyperalert, her thin body crouched close to the ground. She moved a few feet closer, stopping at times to look left and right before finally approaching the saucer of food put out by my husband, Ray.

For a few weeks, Ray and I had known that some animal was coming out of the late fall chill to sleep between our recycling bins. One day when I awoke particularly early, I quietly placed a chair near the porch window and took morning watch there, coffee in hand, hoping to identify our night visitor. Luckily, as dawn's light cleared enough darkness to see, I saw a mass of fur stretch out of its hiding place, revealing a beautiful, gray, long-haired cat. Pausing only to yawn and stretch once more, she headed toward the woods behind our neighbor's house.

Now knowing our guest's identity, Ray began to leave bowls of water and food on the porch before we went to bed. Next, he folded an old towel to soften and warm the cat's nesting space. The fur and empty food bowl left behind confirmed that our visitor remained with us. And as the nights grew colder, Ray's gifts expanded in the form of a heavy cardboard box lined with old towels and wedged into the porch corner unreachable by wind, rain, or frost.

At some point along the way, Ray began to wait on the darkened porch to see if the cat would let him approach. At first, her warrior attitude prevailed; and as soon as she saw him, she hissed, turned, and fled. But after a few nights of this flight and as Ray gently began to call her, she came back to the porch as long as Ray kept his distance. Any "enemy" moves on Ray's part resulted in a fang-bearing hiss and swipe of a paw, claws fully extended. As much as Ray hoped to win her over, this feral or abandoned animal would have none of it, having survived only by stealth, aggression, and distrust of any enemy in her path. When we first met, her fierce warrior nature kept her alive in a threatening world.

Late fall surrendered to early winter, and Ray never abandoned this cat. Every night fresh food and water waited for her, and often Ray would sit, bundled up against the cold, to welcome her from a distance. Little by little, the cat came a bit closer to the man, but any move from him brought out claws and fangs ready to do battle. Still, she came, seeming to grow in trust of both his gifts and his presence. Then one night when Ray came back inside from his watch, he told me that she had rubbed up against his leg. After that, their relationship progressed, always on her terms, but finally to Ray's lap where she began to curl up, sharing warmth against the cold. Only when caught off guard did the fangs and claws of war and instinct come out. Ray's gentleness, patience, and offer of a peaceful coexistence became a way of life between them.

Eleven years later, Ray was the one fighting for survival, at war with life-threatening illnesses that took him into dark and lonely places. Unable to walk without assistance, spending most of his days in a wheelchair or bed, peace of any kind seemed distant. Ray and I hunkered down for the long haul, for the seasons of unrelenting uncertainty brought on by progressive disease. As Ray fought through loss and discouragement, I longed to be his peace-giver, but caregiver fatigue often overwhelmed me while I battled alongside him.

Ray's peace, then, on many days, came through the gift of this once wild warrior-cat. Through years of receiving Ray's unrelenting trustworthiness and gentleness, Cletis (now her name), had moved from porch, to chair, to hearth, and finally to bedside. At first, she served as his work companion, stationing herself on his desk during the day, and when work closed out, taking the night watch on the top of his recliner. Immersed in Ray's peaceful countenance, Cletis assumed a posture of peace in our home, even welcoming guests unconditionally with purrs and caresses.

I watched this transformation over the years, Ray offering and embodying peace to this cat, who at their first meeting struck out for blood if Ray came near. Later when I looked across the den, Cletis could not get close enough to Ray, curled up on his lap or stretched across his chest, warming him, soothing him, reassuring him, and bringing him peace.

When the season for hospice care drew us in, Cletis's loyalty to Ray remained unfaltering. She stayed with him, literally, to the peaceful end of his life, stretching out on his hospital bed so close that we often had to peel her off Ray. She kept watch night and day, nuzzling and pawing every once in a while to let him know she was there for him, just as he had been for her.

Now, from the top of Ray's recliner, Cletis waits and watches for me to come home each day. She has turned her loving attention in my direction, sitting on my lap and stretching out, long and warm, against my side. She helps me remember the peace that Ray brought into my life and into hers. She reminds me that Ray's heart was committed to living as a person of peace, not just with other people but with all of creation. Blessed are the peacemakers in this world. Blessed are the peacemakers of Advent and beyond.

Come quickly, Prince of Peace.

Return to your notebook, journal, or space below to record your responses as you reflect on the following prompts:

- Recall and describe a time in your life where you experienced peace offered by or through another person. Be as specific as you can, remembering where you were and what you were doing at the time.

- Recall a person from your life or lifetime who has been a peacemaker in personal or public ways. Record what you remember about their words and actions. What makes them stand out as a person of peace?

- When have you offered peace to another person or creature? What did you do for him or her? What feelings do you recall from that experience?

DAY THREE

Advent Prayer of Intercession

I want to be at peace, O God,
protector of the frightened,
refuge for the wandering.

I want to speak for peace, O Christ,
hope whispered to the bruised,
welcome sung to the embattled.

I want to live in peace, O Spirit,
forgiveness in my heart,
kindness in my hands;
trusting,
trustworthy;
loving,
beloved.

I want to be at peace, O God,
with you,
with me,
with others.
This is my Advent prayer. Amen.

I invite you to spend more time in Advent prayers of intercession for people in your life and in God's world. Settle into a quiet place for today's exercise that is designed to draw your heart and God's heart closer together through prayer. Become quiet and still, making prayer notes in your notebook, journal, or below as you read each prayer category. At the end of your prayer time, close with a brief time of stillness and silence.

When you are ready, go to God in prayer, reading each intercessory category, and pausing to let your prayers take shape:

Loving God, you ask me to watch and wait for the coming of the Christ child, and in my waiting, you draw me to yourself so that I may become a bearer of your peace and love. Hear my prayers this Advent day as I pray

- for the endangered earth, air, and waters of creation; and for plants and creatures at risk for their very existence.
- for continents, nations, countries, villages, cities, and neighborhoods where people who are at war long for peace.
- for people in my community, congregation, and workplace who experience violence, oppression, and rejection.
- for members of my family and for my friends who struggle every day with personal battles, heartache, or addiction—and who long for inner peace.
- for myself, O God, that I will become a little bolder as a peacemaker and that I may be a little more honest with you about my need for peace in my heart.

DAY FOUR

Read Isaiah 2:1-5, paying careful attention as though it were the first time you have read or heard these words. Then read the words a second time, with an eye and ear for anything that points to God's peace through the text.

> The word that Isaiah son of Amoz saw concerning Judah and Jerusalem. In days to come the mountain of the LORD's house shall be established as the highest of the mountains, and shall be raised above the hills; all the nations shall stream to it. Many peoples shall come and say, "Come, let us go up to the mountain of the LORD, to the house of the God of Jacob; that he may teach us his ways and that we may walk in his paths." For out of Zion shall go forth instruction, and the word of the LORD from Jerusalem. He shall judge between the nations, and shall arbitrate for many peoples; they shall beat their swords into plowshares, and their spears into pruning hooks; nation shall not lift up sword against nation, neither shall they learn war any more. O house of Jacob, come, let us walk in the light of the LORD!

With the Isaiah passage imprinted on your heart, take time now to reflect on the following questions. If you wish, write your reflections in a notebook, journal, or the space below.

As we enter this Advent season, where is war still being learned in God's world? List three or four places and circumstances—personal, local, global, anywhere in creation—where people are being taught ways of war.

Look over what you listed above, and consider *how* war is being learned. Who or what are the "instructors" of war? Who are the "learners"?

Where is God's story about peace in the world being written today? Where is peace being taught and learned this Advent? In particular, where in your community and family is peace being learned?

How can you help God's peace be realized in some small way this Advent?

DAY FIVE

Read Matthew 24:36-44, approaching it as you did the Isaiah text—as though it were brand new to you. If reading aloud is helpful, make use of this practice.

"But about that day and hour no one knows, neither the angels of heaven, nor the Son, but only the Father. For as the days of Noah were, so will be the coming of the Son of Man. For as in those days before the flood they were eating and drinking, marrying and giving in marriage, until the day Noah entered the ark, and they knew nothing until the flood came and swept them all away, so too will be the coming of the Son of Man. Then two will be in the field; one will be taken and one will be left. Two women will be grinding meal together; one will be taken and one will be left. Keep awake therefore, for you do not know on what day your Lord is coming. But understand this: if the owner of the house had known in what part of the night the thief was coming, he would have stayed awake and would not have let his house be broken into. Therefore you also must be ready, for the Son of Man is coming at an unexpected hour."

These verses in Matthew 24 indicate a constant unsettled state for God's people. Phrases including "no one knows," "they knew nothing," "one will be taken and one will be left," "you do not know," and "an unexpected hour" paint a picture of anxiety-brewing vulnerability for the people if they remain passive about the Lord's coming into their lives. What feelings and emotions do these phrases stir up for you?

In this same passage, we receive other words: "Keep awake, therefore," "understand this," and "you also must be ready"—words that can guide us toward a readiness for Christ's coming. These words call for an active waiting, an active expectation of something worth waiting for. What emotions and feelings do these phrases inspire in you?

What do wakefulness, understanding, and readiness have to do with our faith in Emmanuel, God-with-us? How do you use these days of Advent to draw closer to the God of Christmas?

DAY SIX

Praying the Way of Peace

Each year Advent invites us to draw closer to the heart of God. God will again break through to us in scripture, song, and acts of love that we embrace as we approach Christmas.

We cultivate a heart for God and God's people during this season in many ways. One comes through a prayerful reading of Advent scriptures, a spiritual practice named *lectio divina* (sacred reading). *Lectio divina* can teach us to encounter God by engaging God's word through prayer. Today's prayer centers on Isaiah 2:4. Find a quiet place to pray where you will be uninterrupted for ten to fifteen minutes. Then follow the four steps of *lectio divina* listed below.

1. To begin, get comfortable and relaxed, becoming aware of the rhythm of your breath. Relinquish to God any distractions of the day as best you can. Then enter the first reading of the following text, doing so silently or aloud.

> [God] shall judge between the nations, and shall arbitrate for many peoples; they shall beat their swords into plowshares, and their spears into pruning hooks; nation shall not lift up sword against nation, neither shall they learn war any more.

When you have completed this first reading, pause briefly, and then prepare to read the text a second time. In this second reading listen for a word or phrase that captures your attention (resist any analysis about why the word or phrase stands out, just trust what catches your eye or heart). Now begin the second reading; and when the word or phrase becomes clear, stay with it by repeating it silently for a minute or two. Write down your word or phrase below, or in your notebook or journal.

2. The next step of *lectio divina* involves a third reading of the passage. Before you begin to read, focus on these questions: *What feelings, thoughts, sounds, images, or memories come to mind for me through my word or phrase? How does my word or phrase intersect with my life at this time?* Now complete the third reading of the verse. For three minutes or more, make notes about what comes to mind. Do not hurry through this step. Allow God to engage your life through this scripture.

3. The following and third step of *lectio divina* is another and final reading of the scripture. As you read, ask, *"Is there an invitation here for me?"* Through your word or phrase, is God inviting you toward an insight, change, or response in the upcoming days of Advent, especially in this upcoming week? Is this reading, particularly through the word or phrase God draws you toward, nudging you closer to God, to others, to something new? After reading the scripture for the final time, take three or more minutes to reflect on and write down your response.

4. Finally, the last step is to form a prayer, silent or written, asking God to help you receive and respond to the invitation arising from your Advent reading.

DAY SEVEN

Living the Way of Peace

As you close this week's readings, how are you being called through the season of Advent to share God's peace in the world? Begin by responding to the following:

- Where do you need God's peace in your life?

- Where does your family need God's peace?

- Where does your faith community need God's peace?

- Where does your city, town, institution, or village need God's peace?

- Where is God's peace needed in your country or nation?

- What areas of the world need God's peace?

- Where does creation need God's peace?

Prayerfully respond to one of the needs to which your heart and God's heart are called.

Advent Benediction

May the Holy Spirit
forge a new heart in you this Advent—
a heart for peace, not war,
a heart for hope, not fear.
May the stars of the Advent sky
lead you out of darkness into the lap of God
where peace becomes your shelter
and love becomes your home.
Awaken,
be ready,
for the Prince of Peace is coming
to bring peace
to a warring world.
Amen.

WEEK TWO

The Way
of Justice

Justice

DAY ONE

What image comes to mind when you read or hear
the word *justice*?
Write your response in a notebook, journal, or on this page.

Advent Invocation

O, long-sought Justice,
that delicate balance of life and light,
where truth's fulcrum rests
and God's promise pivots.
You are tipped by a mother's first caress
and leveled in the Carpenter's hands.
O Justice,
on your scales
all of heaven and earth
are weighed,
creation,
destruction,
redemption,
Incarnation.
Come, rolling Justice,
come like baptismal waters.
Immerse us
in God's Advent love.
Amen.

Using a notebook, journal, or any space below, complete the following sentences:

- When I consider God's justice, what comes to my mind is

- I long for God's justice when

- God's justice influences my life when

- During Advent and at Christmas, I find God's justice most reflected in

DAY TWO

As you did last week, find a quiet place and time to read the following reflection. To deepen and slow your reading into a more prayerful experience, consider reading aloud.

Three trees have rooted in place beyond the patio wall. To look only where their trunks erupt out of the muddy clay soil would lead me to believe the trees are identical. Each stands as a round, strong column of gray-brown bark, marked by scar-like ridges here and there, as though the tree has sustained some life wounds in the thirty years since its planting. And to the touch, the lower bark tells two sides of life spent in both shade and sun, dark and light—for velvety moss, cool, damp and alive to a fingertip, dapples the side spent in shady darkness. On the sun side—the bark that weathers light, heat, and wind—the outer bark feels tough, hard, and lined like skin left too long in the elements.

Then, just a foot or so from the earth's loving hold, a delightful change takes place in each of the trees. Symmetry and sameness give way to new birth of branches out of the trunk—what began as one living work of creation gives life to two or three—each soundly anchored in the "mother trunk"; but like toddlers taking first steps away from a parent's loving arms, so too these branches lean and curve in many directions, some falling a little toward the earth, others stretching straight up toward the sky. A little higher up, this same life story of new birth and freedom repeats itself, for new branches—uniquely forming in shape and direction yet still tethered to the same life force—shoot off each branch in wild and scattered ways that can be seen only when the thickets of autumn leaves fall away before winter. Until then the branches' life stories remain hidden much like an author's words are hidden until someone opens the book to discover them.

Every year the artistry of autumn leaves drops away from the three trees at the back patio and reveals a story among the trunks and branches. Over time, I have come to understand that they tell stories to be seen by any eyes open to God's authorship about creation as it is intended to be. Sometimes they tell stories of new birth, sometimes of letting go. They offer stories of shelter and other lessons about living through storms. These trees have much to teach about resilience, strength, and beauty—even after part of them has been broken or torn off. And lately I have noticed a story, unexpected but clear, about justice.

Here are three strong trees, fully established and deeply rooted in the ground. Over the years, each has staked a claim for its share of earth, light, and air. Each must drink enough water from the shared soil to support branch, tendril, and leaf. Each must draw up substantial nutrients from the dirt, rotting leaves and sticks, to sustain the "village" that it has become of old growth and stretched-out branches. To a casual passerby the trees might seem "mature" and "set in their ways" of time and space.

But to a more attentive eye, especially in winter, these established mature trees become a prolific storybook by an authoring God who is constantly doing a new thing in the world. And we, God's chosen stewards of creation, can either pay attention and learn how to receive and make room for God's activity in our midst or we can look away.

God's justice creates an opportunity to receive and make room for newness to happen in our midst. To be *just* in the eyes of God is to be fair, equitable, and righteous, engaging in a way of life where all benefit equally and imbalances of power, respect, and sustenance come into right balance. Doing justice, by the standards of our Creator, requires becoming a new creation over and over again so that we fully share all we have and all we are so that all can live together as a new creation. God's justice requires sacrificial living.

And every year and on every branch of the patio trees, God rewrites the story of what the realization of just and shared living requires. First, somewhere between the settled bark and set twigs, a tiny knot appears, disrupting the growth pattern and surface of what already lives along the primary branch. Slowly, daily, the knot grows by tiny increments until a newborn sprout breaks through. And for all the smallness and weakness of the sprout, its tiny existence depends upon sharing sources of sustenance upon which the established tree relies too.

In order to grow into what God intends, in order for new creation to flourish, this tiny needle of a branch must get its share of sun, water, protection, and nourishment as does every other branch on the tree. And the tree, in all its "established" splendor, receives and makes room for new life to be fully shared, even though this means that all other branches will have a little less to live on. Creation is the great equalizer in the world God loves, for all things are created to share what God has given and done. God's justice in all of creation seeks to make this so—seeks to find ways for everything in creation to exist peacefully and live justly.

Sharing room, sharing space, sharing resources so that all of God's creation—humans, plants, animals, earth, sea, sky—can live equitably and fairly as God intends. God's justice requires this of us. May we look for signs of God's new creation in all things this Advent, and may we strive to bear God's justice in the world.

Return to your notebook, journal, or space below to record your responses as you reflect on the following prompts.

- Name an injustice in your local community that you believe breaks God's heart. Jot down a few words about whom this injustice impacts and also what justice would look like in this circumstance.

- Recall a major world event that brought justice to a group of people. How did you find out about this event? What was at stake for the people who longed for justice?

- When have you taken a stand for justice? In as much detail as possible, recall this experience and write it down. Who was involved? What did you do? What was the outcome?

DAY THREE

Advent Prayer of Intercession

I long to bear your justice, O God,
to the captives and captors,
to the bullies and the bullied.

I long to balance my life, O Christ,
to be fair and faithful.
I long to stand with
the falsely accused,
the poorly loved,
the cruelly silenced.

I long to speak your justice, O Spirit,
to sing Mary's song,
to sit with poor shepherds,
to whisper God-with-us,
God-with-us,
Emmanuel.

I long to bear your justice, O God,
to be clothed with mercy
and emboldened by truth.
This is my Advent prayer. Amen.

As this second week of Advent unfolds, allow your own prayers of intercession to form as you think of persons in your life and circumstances in God's world that need prayer. Return to the same quiet place today as you found last week for this exercise. Become quiet and still, making prayer notes in your notebook, journal, or below as you read each prayer category.

When ready, settle into the quiet and read aloud or silently each category below, allowing prayers to come to mind. Do not rush through this time with God.

> Strengthening God, when I make time for you, you teach me your ways of wisdom and truth. Alongside Mary, O Lord, you invite me to ponder all things in my heart, and so I bring to you matters of life in this world that weigh on me when I consider the many needs for justice. Hear my prayers this Advent day as I pray

- for the mistreated water, air, and soil and the many ways that humanity has betrayed your gift of stewardship.
- for continents, nations, countries, villages, cities, and neighborhoods where justice is longed for and people are being treated unjustly.
- for people in my community, congregation, and workplace who experience injustice, prejudice, and discrimination.
- for members of my family and for my friends who struggle every day with unfairness, stereotyping, discrimination, or violence due to injustice.
- for myself, O God, that I may find strength of voice and person to stand up for myself and for those who face injustice at the hands of others. And that I grow in my resolve to become aware of injustices in my community, and to become an instrument of justice wherever I can.

DAY FOUR

Read Isaiah 11:1-10, paying careful attention as though it were the first time you have read or heard these words. Then read it a second time, with an eye and ear for anything that points to God's justice through the text.

A shoot shall come out from the stump of Jesse, and a branch shall grow out of his roots. The spirit of the LORD shall rest on him, the spirit of wisdom and understanding, the spirit of counsel and might, the spirit of knowledge and the fear of the LORD. His delight shall be in the fear of the LORD. He shall not judge by what his eyes see, or decide by what his ears hear; but with righteousness he shall judge the poor, and decide with equity for the meek of the earth; he shall strike the earth with the rod of his mouth, and with the breath of his lips he shall kill the wicked. Righteousness shall be the belt around his waist, and faithfulness the belt around his loins. The wolf shall live with the lamb, the leopard shall lie down with the kid, the calf and the lion and the fatling together, and a little child shall lead them. The cow and the bear shall graze, their young shall lie down together; and the lion shall eat straw like the ox. The nursing child shall play over the hole of the asp, and the weaned child shall put its hand on the adder's den. They will not hurt or destroy on all my holy mountain; for the earth will be full of the knowledge of the LORD as the waters cover the sea. On that day the root of Jesse shall stand as a signal to the peoples; the nations shall inquire of him, and his dwelling shall be glorious.

With the Isaiah passage imprinted on your heart, take time now to reflect on the following questions. If you wish, write your reflections in a notebook, journal, or any of the space below.

In the past year, where have you learned something about "the knowledge of the LORD" in relation to justice? Make specific notes about what you have learned.

As this Advent season points you toward hope, where on earth, nearby or faraway, do you hope to see the wolf living with the lamb or the leopard lying down with the kid as a sign of God's justice? In other words, where might enemies become neighbors through justice being done?

Where are God's people learning about God's justice in your community? How is justice needed in your community? How can you help justice come on earth this Advent?

DAY FIVE

Read Matthew 3:1-12, approaching it, as you did with the Isaiah text, as though it were brand new to you.

> In those days John the Baptist appeared in the wilderness of Judea, proclaiming, "Repent, for the kingdom of heaven has come near." This is the one of whom the prophet Isaiah spoke when he said, "The voice of one crying out in the wilderness: 'Prepare the way of the Lord, make his paths straight.'" Now John wore clothing of camel's hair with a leather belt around his waist, and his food was locusts and wild honey. Then the people of Jerusalem and all Judea were going out to him, and all the region along the Jordan, and they were baptized by him in the river Jordan, confessing their sins. But when he saw many Pharisees and Sadducees coming for baptism, he said to them, "You brood of vipers! Who warned you to flee from the wrath to come? Bear fruit worthy of repentance. Do not presume to say to yourselves, 'We have Abraham as our ancestor'; for I tell you, God is able from these stones to raise up children to Abraham. Even now the ax is lying at the root of the trees; every tree therefore that does not bear good fruit is cut down and thrown into the fire. I baptize you with water for repentance, but one who is more powerful than I is coming after me; I am not worthy to carry his sandals. He will baptize you with the Holy Spirit and fire. His winnowing fork is in his hand, and he will clear his threshing floor and will gather his wheat into the granary; but the chaff he will burn with unquenchable fire."

Our reading today from Matthew's Gospel places us squarely in
view of Jesus' cousin John, a man convinced of Jesus' identity as one
sent from God. Rough in voice and appearance, John holds nothing
back. He brazenly challenges any who will listen that he has come to
fulfill the truth of what the religious leadership has been telling them
all along. John's words will make some cling more fiercely to what
they want to control, but for others he gives a glimpse of hope and
newness for which they long.

How do these words from John the Baptist speak of God's justice that will be made more fully known in Jesus' coming? What do
John's words express about the possibilities of justice for all?

As you consider your baptism and the sacrament of baptism for
all who become members of the body of Christ, in what ways does
baptism speak to you of God's intended justice for the world and
your responsibility as a Christian to be an instrument of justice?

What can you do this Advent, as a baptized member of the body
of Christ, to bear God's justice into a waiting world?

DAY SIX

Praying the Way of Justice

Each year, Advent extends an invitation to draw closer to the heart of God. One way we cultivate a heart for God and God's people is through a prayerful reading of Advent scriptures and the spiritual practice named *lectio divina*. Today's prayer centers on Isaiah 11:1-3. Find a quiet place to pray where you will be uninterrupted for ten to fifteen minutes, and once settled in, again follow the four steps of *lectio divina*.

1. As before, get as comfortable and relaxed as possible, slowing and becoming aware of your breathing. Turn over to God any distractions of the day. One way to do this is to gently acknowledge a distraction but then to imagine placing it aside to be dealt with later. Then begin the first reading of the following text, silently or aloud.

> A shoot shall come out from the stump of Jesse, and a branch shall grow out of his roots. The spirit of the LORD shall rest on him, the spirit of wisdom and understanding, the spirit of counsel and might, the spirit of knowledge and the fear of the LORD. His delight shall be in the fear of the LORD. He shall not judge by what his eyes see, or decide by what his ears hear.

When you have completed this first reading, pause, and then prepare to read the text a second time. In the second reading listen for a word or phrase that captures your attention. (Resist any analysis about why the word or phrase stands out, just trust what stops you or draws you back to it.) Begin the second reading, and when the word or phrase becomes clear, stay with it by repeating it silently for a minute or two. Write down your word or phrase below, or in your notebook or journal.

2. The next step of *lectio divina* is a third reading of the passage. Before you read, focus again on the questions: *What feelings, thoughts, sounds, images, or memories come to mind for me through my word or phrase? How does my word or phrase intersect with my life at this time?* With these questions refreshed in your mind, now read the scripture text a third time, and for three minutes or more make notes about what comes to mind. Do not hurry through this step. As always with prayer, give God time to communicate with you through this scripture.

3. Our third step of *lectio divina* is a final reading of the passage from Isaiah 11. As you read, ask, *"Is there an invitation here for me?"* Through your word or phrase, is God inviting you toward an insight, change, or response in the upcoming days of Advent, especially in this upcoming week? Is this reading, particularly through the word or phrase God has given you, nudging you closer to God, to others, and to something new? Take as much time as you can to allow these questions and the text to sit in your heart and prayers. Should you wish to write down what comes to mind, give yourself time to do so.

4. The last *lectio divina* step is to form a prayer—silent or written—asking God to help you receive and respond to the invitation arising from your Advent reading.

DAY SEVEN

Living the Way of Justice

At the close of this Advent week of readings and prayers, take time on this last day of the week to consider how you may be called through the season of Advent to share God's justice in the world. Begin by taking time to respond to each of the following. Be as specific as you can with each response:

- How is your life influenced by God's justice?

- In what ways does your family life benefit from justice being done?

- How is God's justice lived out and supported by your faith community?

- Who in your city, town, or village longs for God's justice to be realized for them??

- In news from your country or nation, where have you heard of a change being accomplished for justice?

- Name a place in the world where the people cry out for justice.

- How can we "do justice" for the sake of God's creation? Be specific.

Prayerfully select one of the prompts above and discern a way to act in witness, service, or mission during Advent or in the New Year to lend yourself to God's justice somewhere in the world.

Advent Benediction

Bless to us, O God,
your Advent vision
that we may see
with your compassion.

Bless to us, O God,
your Advent heart
that we may love
with holy fairness.

Bless to us, O God,
your Advent soul,
that we may act
with Mary's yes
and let justice
roll down like waters
and righteousness like
an ever-flowing Advent stream.
Amen.

The Way of Fearlessness

Fearlessness

DAY ONE

What image comes to mind when you read or hear
the word *fearlessness?*
Write your response in a notebook, journal, or on this page.

Advent Invocation

Blessed Fearlessness,
wings upon which courage lifts,
faith's great leap toward what is true.
You inspire a maiden's yes,
and convert a shepherd's fear to wonder.
From the lips of angels,
speak to us again,
"Do not be afraid,"
and lead us
beyond fear's darkness
into God's freeing Advent light.
Amen.

Using a notebook, journal, or space below, complete the following sentences:

- When I am afraid, I feel

- God's call to fear not makes me think about

- I can be fearless when

- During Advent and at Christmas, the words of scripture, "Do not be afraid," make me wonder about

DAY TWO

Before reading this reflection, go to a comfortable and quiet place where you will be uninterrupted. As in previous weeks, consider reading this aloud and slowly.

He sat under one of the large awnings near the pool where he was less vulnerable to the day's heat. From there, he could watch everything going on in the water where his friends were cooling off and splashing around. One of the adults who had brought the group of youth to the water park sat on a fold-up camping chair near the young man, pointing out where other members of the group were climbing the diving board ladder or playing on floats and large inner tubes. From a distance, the landlocked conversation seemed enjoyably funny.

Every once in a while, one or more of the group members would climb out of the pool and come to sit with the young man. Soaking wet, his friends would toss beach towels onto the shaded ground near his wheelchair, open cans of beverage, and engage him in conversation. He shook or nodded his head in sync with the inflection of the speaker's words. His long, skinny arms did not have the smooth movement typical for a youth his age; they occasionally jerked and retracted in response to his friends. Then after each swimming break, the youth would get up off their towels, speak to the young man, and head back to the pool.

This went on for several hours—the young man sitting in the shade watching the rest of his group play in the water, adult supervisors taking turns sitting with him under the awning, one or two buddies joining him for conversation; and the cycle would start over. From all evidence, this young man was thoroughly enjoying himself, and the whole scene made it clear that the other group members valued his company. But from a distance I observed that whatever placed him in the wheelchair also kept him out of the pool. His legs and feet never budged, and his arms and head moved rigidly and uncontrollably.

For this young man, even floating would be frightening because he could not communicate or respond in the water if something went wrong, much less move in any way that would protect him. For all the joy the water brought his friends, that same water kept him at a distance. While the others could dive, float, and sink and rise from the bottom of the pool in playful movements, he could do none of this on his own. The pool for the young man was a fearful place.

After a lunch break under the awning, the whole group of young people stretched out in the shade for a while. A few of them encircled the wheelchair and engaged in an animated conversation with the young man seated there. From where I sat, I made out the words, "Come on," paired with a great deal of smiling and laughter. Soon a small huddle formed around the wheelchair, including a couple of the adults. It appeared some plan was underway.

Suddenly a couple of girls from the group ran off toward the pool, while the rest of the group began to peel off t-shirts and flip-flops as they got ready to return to the water. One of the adults helped the youth in the wheelchair take off his t-shirt and put on sunscreen. Like a family of ducks, the whole group began to approach the pool, with the wheelchair leading the way. Near the edge of the water, the adult pushing the chair stopped and knelt in front of its rider, seeming to ask for a final confirmation for the concocted plan.

With apparent approval, another adult slipped into the pool's shallow end where the chair had been guided toward the walk-in steps. The two girls who had disappeared first from lunch waded up to the adult towing a large black inner tube. They pushed the tube to the bottom step and held it in place. Then, with steady strength, an adult leader scooped up the young man from the chair and slowly, steadily carried him down the steps, now lined with the young man's friends, and placed the youth in the inner tube that held him safely above the water while allowing him to feel its refreshing coolness. There the young man floated, surrounded by friends and held safely by the group leaders. His joy was obvious—any fear he felt was gone in the moment, for a love that cast out fear encompassed him.

May we, this Advent, become so buoyed in the joy and love of this season that we look for ways to help others know the steadfast, fearless love of the One who comes to make all things new.

Return to your notebook, journal, or space below to record your responses as you reflect on the following prompts:

- Recall a time in your life when you experienced fear. What were the circumstances? Whom did you turn to for comfort?

- When have you been in position to calm another person's fear? How did you comfort or reassure him or her?

- How does God help you when you feel afraid? Name a specific time in which you turned to God when you felt fear. Take time to describe what happened and how you called on God.

DAY THREE

Advent Prayer of Intercession

I seek to be fearless, God,
to stand against cruel prejudice,
to speak into heartless silence.

I seek to "fear not," O Christ,
to go with you to the leper and to Legion;
to follow you where stones are thrown
and lines are drawn in the sand.

I do not want to be afraid, O Spirit,
I seek courage for my heart,
conviction for my life,
strength for my knees
that I may go where you
beckon me,
call me,
send me.

I seek to be fearless, God,
in love,
in trust,
in faith.
This is my Advent prayer. Amen.

This time of intercessory prayer invites you to remember persons who are frightened and persons who help calm fears. Once again settle into a quiet place for today's prayers that may become an instrument of God's desire to be a source of comfort and trust. Should particular people, needs, or circumstances come to mind that you wish to note in your notebook, journal, or below, give yourself time to do so.

When you are ready, go to God in prayer, reading each intercessory category and pausing to let your prayers take shape.

Comforting God, you send angels to urge us not to be afraid of what is unfolding before us through the birth of the Christ. In awe and wonder, and in confessed fear, we seek your reassurance and comfort. Hear my prayers this Advent day as I pray

- for all creatures great and small who fear capture, abuse, neglect, and extinction; for scientists, ecologists, politicians who fear and fight for the future of our land, water, and air.
- for nations, countries, villages, cities, and neighborhoods where fear runs rampant because of war, unrest, oppression, and poverty.
- for people in my community, congregation, and workplace who face fear because of loneliness, illness, finances, uncertainty, violence, and oppression.
- for members of my family and for my friends who struggle with some level of fear every day—fear of approval or acceptance, fear of failure or of not being good enough.
- for myself, O God, that the fears I harbor in the depths of my soul will come to light in the time that I spend in prayer with you; that you will hold these fears with me and guide me not to fear because you are with me.

DAY FOUR

Today reflect on the prophet Isaiah in the text found in 35:1-10. Take time with the passage, and after some silent reflection, read the text again, keeping "fearlessness" as a lens for your reading.

The wilderness and the dry land shall be glad, the desert shall rejoice and blossom; like the crocus it shall blossom abundantly, and rejoice with joy and singing. The glory of Lebanon shall be given to it, the majesty of Carmel and Sharon. They shall see the glory of the LORD, the majesty of our God. Strengthen the weak hands, and make firm the feeble knees. Say to those who are of a fearful heart, "Be strong, do not fear! Here is your God. He will come with vengeance, with terrible recompense. He will come and save you." Then the eyes of the blind shall be opened, and the ears of the deaf unstopped; then the lame shall leap like a deer, and the tongue of the speechless sing for joy. For waters shall break forth in the wilderness, and streams in the desert; the burning sand shall become a pool, and the thirsty ground springs of water; the haunt of jackals shall become a swamp, the grass shall become reeds and rushes. A highway shall be there, and it shall be called the Holy Way; the unclean shall not travel on it, but it shall be for God's people; no traveler, not even fools, shall go astray. No lion shall be there, nor shall any ravenous beast come up on it; they shall not be found there, but the redeemed shall walk there. And the ransomed of the LORD shall return, and come to Zion with singing; everlasting joy shall be upon their heads; they shall obtain joy and gladness, and sorrow and sighing shall flee away.

Here the prophet Isaiah calls God's people to imagine a future with
God where all their fears will be addressed and turned to joy. In a
time of deeper reflection, use the following questions as your guide,
making notes in your journal or here on the page.

This Advent, who within one hundred miles of your home lives
in fear? List those who come to mind and what it is they may fear.
What do you imagine these persons or communities long for God to
change in their lives and situations that will turn their fear into joy?

Imagine what God's highway, God's Holy Way, would look like.
Use your imagination and all of your senses to describe it. Be as specific as you can.

What does it mean to be "the ransomed of the Lord"? What
would Isaiah have meant when he spoke these words? What does it
mean for us today as we approach Christmas?

DAY FIVE

Read Matthew 11:2-11. Keep the word *fearlessness* in the background of your reading. If reading aloud helps, use this practice as you read a second time.

> When John heard in prison what the Messiah was doing, he sent word by his disciples and said to him, "Are you the one who is to come, or are we to wait for another?" Jesus answered them, "Go and tell John what you hear and see: the blind receive their sight, the lame walk, the lepers are cleansed, the deaf hear, the dead are raised, and the poor have good news brought to them. And blessed is anyone who takes no offense at me." As they went away, Jesus began to speak to the crowds about John: "What did you go out into the wilderness to look at? A reed shaken by the wind? What then did you go out to see? Someone dressed in soft robes? Look, those who wear soft robes are in royal palaces. What then did you go out to see? A prophet? Yes, I tell you, and more than a prophet. This is the one about whom it is written, 'See, I am sending my messenger ahead of you, who will prepare your way before you.' Truly I tell you, among those born of women no one has arisen greater than John the Baptist; yet the least in the kingdom of heaven is greater than he."

The words in Matthew 11 can catch a reader off guard. Why would John question Jesus' being who John claimed he was? And Jesus' response to John's troubling question never receives a definitive answer but points back to John's identity, not that of Jesus. How do these exchanges among John, the disciples, Jesus, and the crowds make you feel when you read them?

In verse 3, what fear lies behind John's question, "Are you the one who is to come, or are we to wait for another?" Be specific in your response.

How does Jesus' reply to John's question quell any fear that John and the disciples may have had about whether Jesus is the Messiah?

Look again at the verses of Matthew 11:2-11 as you consider this question: In what ways, up to this time in their ministries, have the actions of Jesus and his cousin John required them to be fearless for God? What clues does this text reveal about their fearlessness?

DAY SIX

Praying the Way of Fearlessness

Our spiritual practice of *lectio divina* continues to lead us into a prayerful approach to Advent scriptures, thereby guiding us into a deeper relationship with God and God's Word. The rhythm of *lectio* may now be more familiar and comfortable than it was at first. Using the same pattern as in previous weeks, we'll look today at Matthew 11:2-6. Allow ten to fifteen minutes for this practice.

1. Get comfortable and quiet, becoming aware of the rhythm of your breath. In whatever way works best for you, try to set aside other distractions that wrestle for your attention, remembering that you will return to the rest of your day after this time of prayer. Then enter the first reading of the following text, doing so silently or aloud.

> When John heard in prison what the Messiah was doing, he sent word by his disciples and said to him, "Are you the one who is to come, or are we to wait for another?" Jesus answered them, "Go and tell John what you hear and see: the blind receive their sight, the lame walk, the lepers are cleansed, the deaf hear, the dead are raised, and the poor have good news brought to them. And blessed is anyone who takes no offense at me."

After this first reading, pause for a moment or two, and then prepare to read the text a second time. In this second reading listen for a word or phrase that attracts your attention, resisting any judgment or doubt that it is the word or phrase for you. Now begin the second reading. When the word or phrase arises from the reading, stay with it and repeat it silently for a minute or two. Write down your word or phrase below, or in your notebook or journal.

2. You are ready now for the third reading of the scripture passage. The questions for reflection remain the same: *What feelings, thoughts, sounds, images, or memories come to mind for me through my word or phrase? How does my word or phrase intersect with my life at this time?* Now complete the third reading of the passage, and for three minutes or more make notes about what comes to mind. Take your time and invite God to engage your life through this scripture.

3. The fourth and final reading comes next. Read with this question in your heart, *"Is there an invitation here for me?"* Through your word or phrase, is God inviting you toward an insight, change, or response in the upcoming days of Advent, especially in this upcoming week? Is this reading, particularly through the word or phrase God draws you toward, nudging you closer to God, to others, to something new? After reading the scripture for the final time, take three or more minutes to reflect on and write down your response.

4. Finally, the time has come for prayer to take shape from what you have heard, received, or experienced during this practice of *lectio divina* with Matthew 11:2-6.

DAY SEVEN

Living the Way of Fearlessness

As this week draws to a close, take time now to consider ways in which you may be called to live fearlessly as a child of God and follower of Jesus in the world. Make notes if that helps you.

- Where is God calling you not to be afraid in your life?

- Where is God calling you to help someone in your family to "fear not"?

- Where in your faith community does God need you to be fearless?

- What fear in your city, town, institution, or village is on God's heart today? How can you pray for this situation?

- In what ways is your country or nation causing others to be afraid? What needs to happen for this fear to cease?

- Where in God's world is fear turning to joy? Where in God's world is joy turning to fear?

- Where does God's creation require your fearlessness on its behalf?

- Prayerfully respond to one of these needs to which your heart and God's heart feel drawn.

Advent Benediction

May the messengers of God
quell your fears this Advent day—
loosing fear's hold,
softening fear's grip.
May the touch of the Holy Spirit
awaken your desire
to behold the holy
and trust God's promise.
Be ready.
Be waiting.
Prepare
your hearts
to seek God's
joy.
Let it be so.
Amen.

The Way of Faithfulness

Faithfulness

DAY ONE

What image comes to mind when you read or hear
the word *faithfulness?*
Write your response in a notebook, journal, or on this page.

Advent Invocation

Holy Faithfulness,
ancestral home
of every prophet's cry,
eternity's promise
in an infant's whimper.
You are a beam
from the Eastern star
and a quickening
in the human heart.
Pulsing,
beaming,
illumining
God's deepest longing.
Come, O Faithfulness,
labor in us,
be born in us
that we may greet again
the One who comes.
Amen.

Using a notebook, journal, or space below, complete the following sentences:

- To say that God is faithful means

- Faithfulness to God comes most easily to me when

- The spiritual practice that helps me stay faithful to God is

- During Advent and at Christmas, the tradition that draws me closest to the God of my faith is

DAY TWO

As you prepare to read the final reflection of this Advent study, find a comfortable time and place to read and reflect. When ready, begin.

F orgotten" best describes the apartment complex where the women's gathering would take place. Hidden behind more recent commercial buildings that now obscured the two-story row of homes and approachable only by a cracked and crumbling entrance road, the apartments could be taken for abandoned if not for the scattering of bright-colored bikes and riding toys parked near many of the front doors and stairwells.

Up close, the neglected condition of the home exteriors was even more obvious—peeling paint and taped-up windows pocked outer walls. I could see an overfull trash bin across the uneven parking lot, along with a small but oddly neat pile of what looked to be old mattresses and a tangle of broken lamps and small appliances. But once I got out of my car, a closer look at the building revealed freshly swept door stoops and clean window glass where the panes were still whole. And the air, rather than carrying a heavy aroma tamped down with neglect, was saturated with the scent of spices, freshly cooked food, and life.

At the front door of the apartment where the women planned to meet, there were a few pairs of shoes to one side. In fact, I noticed shoes outside most of the apartments—tennis shoes, flip-flops, children's shoes, working boots, and more. Again, these small signs of life were not visible from the road; but for anyone who came close enough to see, they announced the presence of life.

I know before I knock that the community living behind these doors has, for the most part, made its way here from refugee camps in Thailand. Many have fled from Burma through whatever refugee path offered survival and safety. Some have hidden in jungles with children and parents; some have separated from family so that each had a greater chance to make it out of oppressive and dangerous situations. Most have arrived with nothing—no extra clothes, no housewares, little money, and very few personal items. Families of five, six, seven, and more bring a single suitcase with a fraction of their most precious belongings and then crowd into small apartments with other relatives or friends. Their stories are heartbreaking.

I knock, the door opens, and I am immediately ushered into a warm, bright living room that is filled with the aroma of something wonderful coming from the tiny galley kitchen. The few pieces of furniture, old and well-used, are pushed to the edges of the room, leaving a wide-open space on the carpet where I am invited to sit with the other women who have already arrived. They greet me with nods and smiles—the only language we have in common at the moment. As other women arrive at the door, they too slip off their shoes and take a seat on the floor. As varied as the shoes they remove, the clothing of the day mixes traditional Burmese dress with donated t-shirts and skirts, and—for the younger women—elements of the latest fashions. It does not take long until the small apartment is vibrant with laughter and conversation.

A few babies and toddlers join us, freely handed from person to person, as though we are all extended family, which, I realize, we are. We have gathered for the monthly women's Bible study that has been in place for a few years in this or another family apartment. For about twenty minutes, the front door opens and closes while women of many ages slip in and find a place on the carpet, waving or nodding to one another in recognition. Some of them, I notice, carry plastic grocery bags, which they place on the floor when they take a seat. Then our host stands and says something that quiets the group down. In the silence, I realize we are in prayer that I cannot understand but clearly sense. The Bible study, a personal testimony, and more prayer follow, and in the prayer I hear my own name spoken for a brief moment in the language that I do not know.

Immediately two women stand and go to the kitchen to stir the contents of the large pots and pans on the stove. Their movements release more pungent steam into the air, and stacks of small bowls and chopsticks appear on the counter between the kitchen and living room. Distracted momentarily by the kitchen activity, my attention is quickly drawn back to the main gathering where another movement begins. One by one, the women get up from where they are seated and go to a plastic bowl placed on the small coffee table. Each woman drops coins into the bowl, and if she has brought a plastic bag with her, she removes the contents of the bag and places it on the table as well. Out of the bags come baby and children's clothes of every color and condition imaginable: onesies and shirts, blankets and leggings. Some are new, still on hangers, and others look freshly laundered. The pile is not large, but it is present—and a friend sitting near me explains, "For the new family."

These women, who have little, give what they have to the new family who will soon arrive with nothing and enter their community. This is a monthly practice. Each time they gather, the women bring money and gifts for others whom they have never met, others who are wanderers in the world—especially for the babies who will be born to refugee parents of little means. Faithfully, ever so faithfully, these women make room for the alien, the poor, and the vulnerable to experience love incarnate in their midst. May we learn from their faithfulness and love others, as these sisters do, with the love of Christ.

Come, Lord Jesus, enter in so that we may welcome you with all we have this Advent.

Return to your notebook, journal, or space below to record your responses as you reflect on the following prompts:

- Where did you learn to give to others because of your faith? Recall an early experience in your life where someone helped you do this. Who was the person? Who was the recipient?

- Name two or three ways in which you act in faith during the Advent and Christmas holidays. Be specific as you jot these ways down. Review each way that you have noted, and reflect on how each one makes you feel about God when you do it.

- During Advent and approaching Christmas, what is one word that best describes your faith?

DAY THREE

Advent Prayer of Intercession

Help me be faithful, O God,
to receive what awaits me
at the holy manger
and to show others
the way.

Help me be faithful, O Christ,
to hold close the hopeless
and to linger with the lost.

Help me be faithful, O Spirit,
to give voice to the silenced
and manna to the starved.
With the poor,
O Spirit,
let me proclaim
the good news
with my life.

Help me be faithful, O God,
to Christ,
by your Spirit.
This is my Advent prayer. Amen.

As Advent draws toward a close, take time now to extend your prayers for others around God's world. Remembering that God's wide heart can hold all creation, trust that the wideness and depth of your heart can hold the prayers that come to you during this time of intercession. Become quiet and still, making prayer notes in your notebook, journal, or below as you read each prayer category.

Settle into quiet and pray through the prompts listed below. Close with a brief time of stillness and silence.

God of all times and places, you draw me close to you whenever I seek you and make room to be with you. Help me, this day, to broaden my prayers for others and for myself as I seek to grow more faithful to you during this Advent season. I pray

- for the people of your creation, that we may grow more faithful in our care of the earth; that we may grow in our understanding of our interconnectedness to the tiniest of creatures and plants and to the grandest sweep of water and sky.
- for continents, nations, countries, villages, cities, and neighborhoods to be valued and honored by their residents and neighbors so all can find ways to be faithful and respectful of each other and of you.
- for people in my community, congregation, and workplace who come from diverse faith, cultural, ethnic, and political traditions, that we may find ways to live in unity and love.
- for members of my family and for my friends who struggle with their faith because of doubt, spiritual wounds, depression, and other spiritually bruising experiences that keep them from trusting you.
- for myself, O God, that the scriptures, prayers, and worship of this Advent season will spark in my faith a new hope in the promise you have made to us through Christ our Savior.

DAY FOUR

Our reading from the prophet this day comes from Isaiah 7:10-16. Consider each word and phrase for what it may bring to your mind and heart. Read slowly in silence, as though these words are spoken to you today. Then, read the text aloud as if a friend were listening to it for the first time.

Again the LORD spoke to Ahaz, saying, Ask a sign of the LORD your God; let it be deep as Sheol or high as heaven. But Ahaz said, I will not ask, and I will not put the LORD to the test. Then Isaiah said: "Hear then, O house of David! Is it too little for you to weary mortals, that you weary my God also? Therefore the Lord himself will give you a sign. Look, the young woman is with child and shall bear a son, and shall name him Immanuel. He shall eat curds and honey by the time he knows how to refuse the evil and choose the good. For before the child knows how to refuse the evil and choose the good, the land before whose two kings you are in dread will be deserted.

Now take time to reflect on what you read, saw, and heard in the Isaiah text today. Use all of your senses—sight, touch, smell, hearing, tasting—to help you experience the passage with your full being as you respond to the following questions.

As you read this text, imagine that you are a bystander overhearing Ahaz and the Lord. Describe God's voice as you imagine it to be in this exchange. Once you have done so, do the same for the voice of Ahaz. What adjectives come to mind? what emotions?

Now approach the scene in your imagination again through your senses. What do you see in the scene? What sounds do you hear? List them. What aromas come to your nostrils? Do you experience a sense of flavors and tastes? What surfaces or textures would you touch in the scene if you were present?

This text from Isaiah points to a sign of "the young woman will be with child." Throughout Advent, for us the image of a young, expectant Mary is a common reminder of the Christmas story. What feelings does this image evoke in you?

DAY FIVE

On this fifth day of the last week of Advent, prayerfully read the Gospel text of Matthew 1:18-25. As with the Isaiah reading, first read silently, then aloud, trusting that God has something here for you to receive.

> Now the birth of Jesus the Messiah took place in this way. When his mother Mary had been engaged to Joseph, but before they lived together, she was found to be with child from the Holy Spirit. Her husband Joseph, being a righteous man and unwilling to expose her to public disgrace, planned to dismiss her quietly. But just when he had resolved to do this, an angel of the Lord appeared to him in a dream and said, "Joseph, son of David, do not be afraid to take Mary as your wife, for the child conceived in her is from the Holy Spirit. She will bear a son, and you are to name him Jesus, for he will save his people from their sins." All this took place to fulfill what had been spoken by the Lord through the prophet: "Look, the virgin shall conceive and bear a son, and they shall name him Emmanuel," which means, "God is with us." When Joseph awoke from sleep, he did as the angel of the Lord commanded him; he took her as his wife, but had no marital relations with her until she had borne a son; and he named him Jesus.

On so many levels, the theme of faithfulness weaves through this passage. First, there is Mary's faithfulness to God, but there is also her faithfulness (although at first doubted) to her betrothed, Joseph. As you read through the remainder of the text, verses 19-25, list other acts or responses to faithfulness that appear or are implied in this scripture.

Recall a time in your life or in the life of another when a decision that appeared illogical to most people was grounded in faithfulness to God.

Beginning with "Emmanuel," write a brief prayer asking God-with-us to help you grow in trust and love of God during this Advent and Christmas season.

DAY SIX

Praying the Way of Faithfulness

In this final week of Advent, allow the spiritual practice of *lectio divina* to again help you draw even closer to God through praying the scriptures. Throughout this study, you have practiced different ways to expand your heart for God. Today will be no different.

1. Our practice of *lectio divina* today invites you to focus on Matthew 1:20*b*-25. Begin your sacred reading as you have before, in a quiet space where you can spend time with God and the text. Remember that your first reading simply acquaints you with the passage through a silent reading.

> An angel of the Lord appeared to him in a dream and said, "Joseph, son of David, do not be afraid to take Mary as your wife, for the child conceived in her is from the Holy Spirit. She will bear a son, and you are to name him Jesus, for he will save his people from their sins." All this took place to fulfill what had been spoken by the Lord through the prophet: "Look, the virgin shall conceive and bear a son, and they shall name him Emmanuel," which means, "God is with us." When Joseph awoke from sleep, he did as the angel of the Lord commanded him; he took her as his wife, but had no marital relations with her until she had borne a son; and he named him Jesus.

Pause for a minute or two, then begin your second reading of this text from Matthew's Gospel, listening for the word or phrase that rises up to meet you in the reading—the word or phrase that catches your heart or mind in some way. When you have finished the second reading, write down or hold in memory your word or phrase and let it settle into your thoughts for another minute or two, meditating on what has stayed with you before you enter your third reading.

2. To prepare for the third reading of the passage, read over these questions: *What feelings, thoughts, sounds, images, or memories come to mind for me through my word or phrase? How does my word or phrase intersect with my life at this time?* When ready, read the scripture for the third time, remaining open to ways in which the reading may intersect with your life today. Remember that this time is prayerful time, time to receive what God may want for you through the reading. Take your time—three to five minutes at least—and remain open, cultivating a heart for God as you do.

3. When you are ready, prepare for the fourth and final reading of the scripture passage from Matthew. In this reading, you ask, *"Is there an invitation here for me?"* Perhaps your word or phrase will point you toward an invitation from God to act, pray, change, or respond to something in your life or the world. Perhaps the rest of the scripture has brought new insight or challenge to you, inviting you to turn prayerfully in a new direction. Or, perhaps this time in prayer has helped you open God's invitation to remember that you are loved. Read the scripture, then take all the time you need to reflect on and write down both the invitation you hear and any response you sense in your heart.

4. Close this time of sacred reading—of praying the scripture—in prayer. Write in your journal, notebook, or on the contours of your heart.

DAY SEVEN

Living the Way of Faithfulness

How does God's faithfulness to creation show in the world today? How is humanity shaped and called to be faithful to God? Where do you experience God's call to grow in faithfulness so that your faith in God-with-us can bring light to a waiting world? Reflect on and respond through the questions below.

- Where do you see evidence of God's faithfulness to you?

- How do you practice faithfulness to God as a member of your family?

- In what ways does your faith community practice faithfulness to God?

- In your city, town, institution, or village, what groups of faithful people are making a difference?

- How does your faithfulness to God make a difference for you as a citizen of your country or nation?

- Where is God's faithfulness at work in the world?

- How can you live out your faithfulness to God by caring for creation?

Prayerfully respond to one of these needs to which your heart and God's heart are called.

Advent Benediction

As this day ends,
God—who is faithful—will rest with you.
As this day ends,
Christ—who is faithful—will rest in you.
As this day fades away,
the Spirit—who is faithful—will never leave you.
As it was in the beginning,
as it awaits you at the manger,
as it is promised on Christmas Day,
the faithful love of God will be yours
now and always.
Let it be so.
Amen.

Leader's Guide

Begin this study the week before the first Sunday of Advent.

Before the Group Gathers

This small-group study can function for either a sixty- or ninety-minute session with eight or more participants. It will be best if the small-group sessions begin on a day before the first Sunday of Advent, but it does not matter which day of the week the group meets. Participants will prepare for each weekly session by following the daily readings in *Prepare the Way: Cultivating a Heart for God in Advent*.

To prepare for the first week of reading, participants will read Day One seven days before the first group session and Day Seven on the day of the small-group meeting, before the group session. This same reading pattern will continue, Day One being read the day after the group session and Day Seven on the day of but before the group session. Participants will need their copy of *Prepare the Way* at least a full week before the first group session, along with instructions (e-mail or text) for how to prepare for the first session. The leader may prefer to schedule an introductory group session to hand out books, make introductions, and give instructions.

For each group session, participants will need their copies of *Prepare the Way* as well as something to write in (notebook, journal, tablet). The leader needs to communicate clearly the full schedule for the group as well as the location for the group sessions, parking instructions if applicable, and encouragement for weekly punctuality. Make name tags or name cards for all participants, depending upon whether you will sit at tables.

[Optional] A small Advent wreath may be used during this study. If the leader chooses to do so, he or she will identify or label each of the four Advent candles as follows: Peace, Justice, Fearlessness, and Faithfulness. Also, a candlelighter will be needed each week.

[Optional] If a ninety-minute small-group format is being followed, one option involves identifying an Advent or Christmas hymn that reflects the word of the week (such as *Peace, Justice*, and so on) and inviting participants to reflect upon the lyrics and message of the hymn. This activity will require hymnals or copies of the hymn.

WEEK ONE

Peace

Gathering and Welcome [3–5 minutes]

Call to Community [5 minutes]

- The leader checks in with group participants asking: How was this week's reading for you?

- Lighting of the Advent Candle(s) [Optional, 1 minute] The leader says, while lighting one candle, "We light this candle, reflecting on God's call to be people of peace."

Prayer of Invocation [1–2 minutes]

- All turn to page 18 and read the Advent Invocation together.

Scripture Reading and Reflection—The Prophet
[15 minutes]

- The leader invites participants to form triads, instructing them to read together Isaiah 2:1-5 and then discuss their responses from page 27.

90-minute format only

- Break [5 minutes]
- Return to triads and reflect on responses to Day One sentence completions [10 minutes]
- Return to full group and turn to Day Three (page 25). The leader guides a brief discussion asking participants to share

any prayers that arose using these prayer categories. [15 minutes]

- *OR the leader may choose to identify an Advent or Christmas hymn that references peace and to lead a discussion about the lyrics and message.*

Continue with 60- or 90-minute format

Scripture Reading and Reflection—The Gospel
[10 minutes]

- In the full group, the leader asks a volunteer to read aloud Matthew 24:36-44, and then guides a discussion using the questions on page 29.

Living the Way of Peace [15 minutes]

- All turn to Day Seven (pages 32–33), and the leader asks participants to identify the question that prompted a response they plan to follow up with. As time permits, participants may identify more than one way they will live the way of peace.

Benediction [1 minute]

- All turn to page 34 and read the Advent Benediction in unison.

WEEK TWO

Justice

Gathering and Welcome [3–5 minutes]

Call to Community [5 minutes]

- The leader checks in with group participants asking: How was this week's reading for you?

- Lighting of the Advent Candle(s) [Optional, 1 minute]
  The leader says, while lighting two candles, "We light these candles, reflecting on God's call to be people of justice and peace."

Prayer of Invocation [1–2 minutes]

- All turn to page 38 and read the Advent Invocation together.

Scripture Reading and Reflection—The Prophet
[15 minutes]

- The leader invites participants to form triads, instructing them to read together Isaiah 11:1-10 and then discuss their responses from page 47.

90-minute format only

- Break [5 minutes]
- Return to triads and reflect on responses to Day One sentence completions [10 minutes]
- Return to full group and turn to Day Three (page 45). The leader guides a brief discussion asking participants to share

any prayers that arose using these prayer categories. [15 minutes]

- *OR the leader may choose to identify an Advent or Christmas hymn that references justice and lead a discussion about the lyrics and message.*

Continue with 60- or 90-minute format

Scripture Reading and Reflection—The Gospel
[10 minutes]

- In the full group, the leader asks a volunteer to read aloud Matthew 3:1-12, and then guides a discussion using questions on page 49.

Living the Way of Justice [15 minutes]

- All turn to Day Seven (pages 52–53), and the leader asks participants to identify the question that prompted a response they plan to follow up with. As time permits, participants may identify more than one way they will live the way of justice.

Benediction [1 minute]

- All turn to page 54 and read the Advent Benediction in unison.

WEEK THREE

Fearlessness

Gathering and Welcome [3–5 minutes]

Call to Community [5 minutes]

- The leader checks in with group participants asking: How was this week's reading for you?

- Lighting of the Advent Candle(s) [Optional, 1 minute]
  The leader says, while lighting three candles, "We light these candles, reflecting upon God's call to 'not be afraid' and to be people of justice and peace."

Prayer of Invocation [1–2 minutes]

- All turn to page 58 and read the Advent Invocation together.

Scripture Reading and Reflection—The Prophet
[15 minutes]

- The leader invites participants to form triads, instructing them to read together Isaiah 35:1-10 and then discuss their responses from page 66.

<u>90-minute format only</u>

- Break [5 minutes]
- Return to triads and reflect on responses to Day One sentence completions [10 minutes]
- Return to full group and turn to Day Three (page 64). The leader guides a brief discussion asking participants to share

any prayers that arose using these prayer categories. [15 minutes]

- *OR the leader may choose to identify an Advent or Christmas hymn that references fearlessness and lead a discussion about the lyrics and message.*

Continue with 60- or 90-minute format

Scripture Reading and Reflection—The Gospel
[10 minutes]

- In the full group, the leader asks a volunteer to read aloud Matthew 11:2-11, and then guides a discussion using questions on page 68.

Living the Way of Fearlessness [15 minutes]

- All turn to Day Seven (pages 71–72), and the leader asks participants to identify the question that prompted a response they plan to follow up with. As time permits, participants may identify more than one way they will live the way of fearlessness.

Benediction [1 minute]

- All turn to page 73 and read the Advent Benediction in unison.

WEEK FOUR

Faithfulness

Gathering and Welcome [3–5 minutes]

Call to Community [5 minutes]

- The leader checks in with group participants asking: How was this week's reading for you?

- Lighting of the Advent Candle(s) [Optional, 1 minute]
  The leader says, while lighting four candles, "We light these candles, reflecting on God's call to faithfulness and to 'not be afraid.' We light these candles in response to God's call to be people of justice and peace."

Prayer of Invocation [1–2 minutes]

- All turn to page 78 and read the Advent Invocation together.

Scripture Reading and Reflection—The Prophet
[15 minutes]

- The leader invites participants to form triads, instructing them to read together Isaiah 7:10-16 and then discuss their responses from page 87.

90-minute format only

- Break [5 minutes]
- Return to triads and reflect on responses to Day One sentence completions [10 minutes]
- Return to full group and turn to Day Three (page 85). The leader guides a brief discussion asking participants to share any prayers that arose using these prayer categories. [15 minutes]
- *OR the leader may choose to identify an Advent or Christmas hymn that references faithfulness and lead a discussion about the lyrics and message.*

Continue with 60- or 90-minute format

Scripture Reading and Reflection—The Gospel
[10 minutes]

- In the full group, the leader asks a volunteer to read aloud Matthew 1:18-25, and then guides a discussion using the questions on page 89.

Living the Way of Faithfulness [15 minutes]

- All turn to Day Seven (pages 92–93), and the leader asks participants to identify the question that prompted a response they plan to follow up with. As time permits, participants may identify more than one way they will live the way of faithfulness.

Benediction [1 minute]

- All turn to page 94 and read the Advent Benediction in unison.

About the Author

PAMELA C. HAWKINS is an author, artist, and pastor living in Nashville, Tennessee. She has written about the Christian spiritual life through prayers, liturgies, articles, small-group studies, and devotional books. At the heart of Hawkins's ministry is a love for the gospel, a commitment to extend God's unconditional love to all people, and a desire to live a more prayerful life. Hawkins holds a Master's of Divinity degree from Vanderbilt University Divinity School, a Doctor of Ministry in Christian Spirituality from Columbia Theological School, and is a regular retreatant at the Benedictine community of St. Meinrad Archabbey.

CPSIA information can be obtained at www.ICGtesting.com
Printed in the USA
LVOW10s2010240616

494060LV00003B/6/P